About the Author

Lesley Mukwacha is a nature conservationist, storyteller, film script writer, music producer, song writer and musician who loves travelling, meeting and making new friends from all around the world. He lives mostly in Zimbabwe's capital city of Harare, although he comes from the small resort town of Kariba. He led international travellers from Cape Town to Uganda, mostly in overland trucks custom made to carry around twenty-two passengers, buses, and 4x4 vehicles, through Namibia, South Africa, Botswana, Zimbabwe, Zambia, Malawi, Tanzania, Mozambique, Kenya and Rwanda.

African Tour Leader's Campfire Tales

Lesley Mukwacha

African Tour Leader's Campfire Tales

Olympia Publishers
London

www.olympiapublishers.com
OLYMPIA PAPERBACK EDITION

Copyright © Lesley Mukwacha 2024

The right of Lesley Mukwacha to be identified as author of
this work has been asserted in accordance with sections 77 and 78 of
the Copyright, Designs and Patents Act 1988.

All Rights Reserved

No reproduction, copy or transmission of this publication
may be made without written permission.
No paragraph of this publication may be reproduced,
copied or transmitted save with the written permission of the publisher,
or in accordance with the provisions
of the Copyright Act 1956 (as amended).

Any person who commits any unauthorised act in relation to
this publication may be liable to criminal
prosecution and civil claims for damage.

A CIP catalogue record for this title is
available from the British Library.

ISBN: 978-1-80439-713-8

This is a work of fiction.
Names, characters, places and incidents originate from the writer's
imagination. Any resemblance to actual persons, living or dead, is
purely coincidental.

First Published in 2024

Olympia Publishers
Tallis House
2 Tallis Street
London
EC4Y 0AB

Printed in Great Britain

Dedication

I dedicate this book to all the travellers that have been led by me through Africa.

Acknowledgements

Thank you to Patricia Bakker for helping with financing the initial publication of this book; Kembo Sithole, my friend for many years, who listened to all my stories and advised me without bias; and, last but not least, Diana Devito, for reading my stories, giving me words of encouragement and offering advice and ideas.

Chapter 1
Me Against the Lions

Zimbabwe's Hwange National Park is one of the best wildlife sanctuaries in Africa. It is home to the Big Five, and getting a job as a guide in one of the best lodges there was a dream come true for me. The three months I had worked there had been nothing but exciting, as I also had the chance to work with some of the best guides in the field. I was going to enjoy working here. My clients for the next four days would be three Japanese young men that I had picked up from the small airport about ten kilometres from the lodge.

They were so happy to finally set foot in Africa. As we drove from the airport, they made it very clear that the only animal they were interested in seeing was the lion, especially a large maned one. I had responded with a smile on my face, assuring them that I would do my best to find them what they wished to see, even though, inwardly, I was saying, "They are wild animals in a big national park; finding them is no easy walk in the park." That night, I thought about the route I was going to take; the watering holes I was going to visit. I would start with a drive up to the closest watering hole where I had been lucky with some cats a few days before, look for lion footprints, and if I found some, our walking safari would begin there.

At five thirty a.m. sharp, I was done loading up the cooler box with our refreshments: coffee, tea, and sandwiches for our breakfast and light lunch while on the safari. With my 458 magnum in the passenger seat next to me, my safari hat and sunglasses on the dashboard, I waited for the arrival of my clients from their rooms. When I glanced at my big game hunting gun next to me, I wondered if I ever was going to use it one day. I remembered our manager's answer the previous night to one of the other client's questions during dinner, and a nerve twitched at the back of my neck.

"But if guides carry guns on safaris," the client had said, "why do we hear of some of them being killed by animals?"

"Well," the manager had answered, "imagine being on a safari with a seemingly very experienced, knowledgeable guide, and within the first five minutes of your safari, you are staring down at an elephant or lion or rhino, or leopard that he has just shot and killed. Even if you knew that it was for your protection, it just wouldn't seem right. So, guides wait until the very last moment, praying that it's just a mock charge; and if it turns out not to be, it may be too late. And more often than not, it is the guide who dies coz he is always positioned between his clients and danger." With a heavy sigh, the client had nodded in agreement.

My clients arrived, said good morning to me before hopping onto the open roof 4x4, and, I was about to turn on the engine, when Jonas, one of the trainee guides who had been helping with the preparation of lunch packs in the kitchen, ran up to us, signalling for me to wait. "Lesley," he said, "I think I heard lions last night by my tent. They might still be close by." I couldn't believe my ears. I jumped off my seat, told my clients to remain in the car, and walked with Jonas back to his tent. There were fresh lion footprints, for sure. There could easily have been ten lions. My heart beating excitedly, I hurried back to the 4x4.

"Guys," I said, "we may as well start our walk here." I

snatched my rifle from the passenger seat and waited for them to gather their small backpacks and cameras, and together we headed back to the lions' spoor.

Standing in front of them, I gently but firmly reminded them, "Guys, remember our briefing last night, should we get charged by any dangerous animal, do not run. Wait for my instructions. Got it?"

I looked around at all three of them and smiled when they all said, "Got it, Lesley." We began our walk, me in front and them in a single file behind me. After walking for about five minutes, occasionally pausing to listen carefully for any noises, I saw a clearing on the ground where the lions seemed to have laid down for a bit. I crouched down and placed the back of my hand against the ground. It felt warm, a sign that they had just left.

I looked up at the guys and whispered, "They just left. Keep your eyes open."

From that crouched position, I carefully scanned the area around us, saw nothing, and rose to my feet. The tall yellow grass all over the area made it difficult to see anything. Having a better sense of smell and hearing than us, most wild animals notice us long before we see them, and more often than not, if they are not territorial, they will move away, avoiding confrontation, but if they are territorial, the likes of leopards, black rhino, hippos, and black mamba, your journey to heaven or hell, may be a very short one. They protect their territories. Lions have home ranges instead of territories, so usually, they move away, but only for so long, before they get pissed off.

We set off again, this time a lot more slowly than before. We had only done a few hundred yards when a movement about three hundred metres ahead of us, by a big acacia bush, caught my eye. I stopped, signalling with my right hand, for the guys behind me to do the same. I could feel my fingers tightening around my rifle. A couple of ears appeared above the grass and suddenly, I knew they were lions. I could count about five pairs of ears. They were staring at us. Very softly, I said, "Guys, lions, under that bush." I was pointing at the bush.

The clients started getting their big cameras ready. The loud clicking noises as they fitted the appropriate lenses were slowly getting on my nerves and making me nervous, but there was nothing I could do. They wanted to see lions, and they surely wanted to take pictures. Then, without warning, a growling female lion shot out of the bush in a terrifying charge that shook the ground beneath my feet. In what seemed like a split second, she was standing about fifteen metres in front of us, her eyes bloodshot and her white-tipped tail swishing from side to side – a sign that "I'm very agitated and still thinking about my next move". The growling did not stop, and the red eyes did not leave mine for a second.

With my rifle raised and aimed at its head, I was thinking fast. Should I pull the trigger, or should I not? Behind me, there was total silence; all I could hear was my own breathing below the menacing growl and grunts from the lioness. In almost a whisper, and without turning my head, I spoke to my clients, "Guys, whatever you do, don't run." I wasn't expecting any audible response, and I got none. When a lion stands in front of you, its canines showing in that unholy grin, a lot of muscles seize to function. The knees turn to jelly, the mouth goes dry, and your neck stiff – the only thing one can do is pray silently; no muscles are needed there.

We stared at each other for what seemed like an eternity before the tail-swishing slowed down and the growls turned to soft terrifying grunts. She laid down on her belly. That is when I told myself if we were to move, this was the time. She seemed a bit calm and composed now. So, without turning around, I started backing up slowly, whispering to the guys behind me, "Guys, let's back up slowly." The lion didn't move, it just stopped grunting and continued to stare at me.

I also noticed that her eyes were no longer as red as they were before. "Don't get your hopes high yet," I told myself as I continued to slowly and quietly back away, my rifle rigid in my grip. At some point, I thought the lioness looked around me at the guys behind and turned to look at the other lions over by the bush. From the corner of my eye, I saw tiny little ears among the big ones and understood. There were cubs. This made them more dangerous.

I think I had put about fifty yards between me and the lioness when, suddenly, she got up and walked slowly back to the pride. It was as if the other lions had just told her to leave the poor guys alone. I waited for her to reach the pride before I could turn around. As I watched, two large males got out of the bush and stretched, yawning as they rubbed up against each other. Assuring myself that we were now safe, I heaved a sigh of relief, lowered my rifle, and turned around. Cold sweat broke out all over my body. For a moment, I forgot about the lions, and terror gripped me upon realising that the Japanese had varnished. When and how, I had no idea. It suddenly dawned on me that all along I had been alone and talking to myself. The lioness must have been laughing at me, in its mind going like, "Who the hell you talking to, the boys are gone."

That's probably the look I had seen in her eyes when she looked around me and at the other lions, probably laughing and mocking me. Shaking my head in utter disbelief, I started walking back to the lodge. Realising that I had been alone against a possible pride of ten lions was more frightening than the actual charge. Because we hadn't gone more than two kilometres from the lodge, in about fifteen minutes I was back. Up until now, I haven't gotten over the fact that the clients hadn't even alerted the management to what had happened. They were just sitting by the pool, and when they saw me, they jumped to their feet and approached me, murmuring, "Lesley, are you okay?"

I was speechless. I just managed to shrug before proceeding to my manager's office.

If the lions had decided to attack me and I had tried to fight back, eventually they would have overpowered me because nobody was coming; no one had been informed. That alone still sends shivers down my spine.

The clients spent the next three days at the lodge, in the swimming pool, bar, and in hammocks, reading books or playing cards. No one wanted anything to do with game viewing any more. They had seen enough lions.

Chapter 2
Glowing Eyes in the Dark

Having a well-travelled someone as a client on a group tour of twenty people can be your worst nightmare, especially if they claim to know everything, and do exactly the opposite of what you ask them to do. It happened to me on several occasions, but out of all these, one particular incident tops them all.

    I was leading a forty-four-day overland trip from Cape Town to Nairobi a couple of years ago and had the nicest group of young travellers who were so happy and excited to be on such a tour for the first time in their lives. Their dream had finally come true. Their guide was the best. He spoke fluent English and seemed very knowledgeable that within the first five minutes of the first briefing, they had become comfortable and confident that they had booked the best trip, with the best tour company; and they were right. The excitement showed in their eyes as they listened to me brief them on how the tour was going to be.

As I spoke, I was a bit worried about the absence of one guy I had met early on in the hotel lobby. He had seen our company logo on my t-shirt and approached me, his hand outstretched for a handshake.

"You must be Lesley, the guide on my Cape to Nairobi?" he had said with a half-smile on his face. From the accent, I could tell he was Australian.

Taking his hand, I said, "Yes, that is me. How do you do?"

"I'm doing great, actually. Been exploring the city the whole morning. I like it," he had said that with a slight nod of his head.

I had only a few hours to do food shopping for the tour and be ready for the briefing that evening such that I did not have a lot of time to chat with him. I kindly reminded him of the briefing at six p.m., in the conference room by the reception area, to which his worrying response had been, "Well, I have been to so many meetings of this nature before and I still need to do a bit more sightseeing. I might be late, so please don't wait for me."

Without waiting for my response, he had walked off. He still had not yet arrived, fifteen minutes into the briefing. Just as I was about to ask if anyone had any questions, he walked in, waving at the other clients with a big smile on his face. I continued with the briefing, and when I was done, I looked over at him and said, "Departing time tomorrow is at eight a.m." Since he had been to so many briefings, I guessed departure time was all that mattered to him.

The first seven-eight days of the trip went smoothly, as we did not have a lot of rules to worry about. Let us call this guy

Phil. True to his word, this guy was well-travelled and well-read. He seemed to know everything, about how to find and catch scorpions, snakes, and butterflies. I had kindly warned him of the dangers associated with catching poisonous creatures on a tour like this one, but his response had told me to back off.

On this particular trip, we drive for days in remote areas and deserts, with no hospitals nearby, such that should you get beaten by the likes of the notorious black mamba, the cape cobra, or the thick-tailed scorpion, you are faced with imminent death. But then again, this guy knew everything, so, against my better judgement, I let him be. Things started to get worse halfway through Namibia when he started just disappearing from camp, returning later with beautiful pictures of more and more potentially dangerous creatures, and sometimes he would go with some of the clients. At one point, I decided I had had enough. I called him aside and had a serious talk with him. I told him not to endanger the lives of the other clients, and I strongly warned him against pushing me to the point where I would be forced to throw him off the tour. He did not like it, but he had known I was not bluffing. So, reluctantly, he apologised and became very quiet and withdrawn from then on.

Now, surprisingly, when you do good, there are always some people who actually hate you for that, no matter how much you explain your actions to them. Several clients seemed unhappy with me. One lady even said to me, "That was wrong. That guy paid to enjoy this trip. You should go easy on him."

I just looked at her and kept my mouth shut, for if I had opened it, I probably would have made one more enemy on this trip. Namibian national parks' campsites are all fenced in, and that way, dangerous animals are kept out, except, of course, for snakes that can easily crawl under the fence. On game drives, no one is allowed off the vehicles except in specially designated areas called picnic spots, so that made things a bit easy for me. Trouble started again when we entered the Ngorongoro Crater National Park in Tanzania. The campsites there are not fenced in, and animals can walk through any time they see fit. I had to keep a much closer eye on Phil.

After dinner at the only public campsite at Ngorongoro, I told everyone at the briefing to be very careful, especially at night. This was the land of the Big Five, and even walking without a torch at night was not advised. If anyone had to use the bathroom, for number one, rather just do it by your tent, for number two, wake someone up and go in a group of two or three. Use a torch at all times at night. If need be, wake me up from the roof of the truck, where I slept. They had all nodded consent, and when we all finally went to sleep, a tingling sensation at the back of my neck told me something sinister was going to happen tonight.

Somewhere in the middle of the night, a single loud scream woke me up with a start.

I rolled over to one side and fumbled for my big flashlight. As I shone the light over by the toilets, the beam fell on what seemed like a person lying on the ground. My heart suddenly pounding, I reached over the side of the cab and opened the driver's side door. I got in without touching the ground, turned on the engine, and blared the horn. The plan was to wake as many people in the camp as possible. It worked. In less than three minutes, people were coming out of their tents, torches shining, and coming up to my truck. All my clients also came, and the usual questions started coming. "What's happening? What's the matter?"

I told everyone what I had seen and together we cautiously approached the toilets.

I had been right. It indeed was a man. He was lying on the

grass, unconscious, and had on just a pair of boxer shorts. I knelt beside him, and, careful not to harm him more, I rolled him over, and my heart skipped a bit. It was Phil. His eyes seemed lifeless, his whole face pale, and he had only a very faint pulse on his arm. I looked for any kind of wound on his body but found none. Because it was freezing cold, I asked some guys to help me carry him to our kitchen, where it was slightly warmer and we could try and administer first aid. The guys helped me carry him.

A few moments after making him warm with several blankets, he came round. His eyes searched around for anyone he could recognise and finally landed on me.

Slowly realising what was happening, he spoke very softly to me and fell back to sleep. His words were, "I'm sorry, man. I'm so sorry."

Three other guys and I stayed with him in that kitchen until sunrise. We were waiting to be briefed. This is what had happened.

Sometime after midnight, when everybody had fallen asleep, Phil had to go take a piss. But because he hated following rules, instead of doing it just by his tent, he had gone to the toilet. He had no intention of going inside, he just liked the idea of doing exactly the opposite of what I had said. It was pitch black that night, and if you held your hand more than thirty centimetres in front of your eyes, you could not see it. Satisfied that where he stood was the best spot to let fly, he pushed down the top of his boxer shorts and was about to hang it out when he saw two large glowing eyes by the ground slightly to his right. His mischievous mind working fast, he turned, aimed between the two eyes, and released.

I know this may sound crazy, but it is true. Men love to aim at things when urinating. If you do not want them splashing all over the toilet seat, put a tiny blackish object inside and see. I remember some years back when I visited a friend in Europe, at Charles De Gaulle Airport in France, they had tiny black imitations of black flies in the urinal to keep man from messing everywhere else. So, Phil, without being provoked, had taken aim between those eyes on the ground, looked up into the sky, and viewed the stars.

When he was done, he did the shake shake, before looking down at the eyes; they were not there any more; instead, they were right in front of his own eyes.

Right away he knew this was no small wild cat. This was a large animal. Fear gripped him and as he fell back, he let out a yell that had woken me up and passed out. Probably wondering, "What the hell?" The animal had turned and walked away.

When later that morning we went back to check the place where it had happened, we were shocked at our discovery. Phil had pissed between the eyes of the most dangerous of the Big Five; the ever pissed-off Cape water buffalo. There can only be one explanation for the buffalo's behaviour. Most animals I know of in the antelope and Bovidae family enjoy salt. The salty taste of urea in his urine probably saved him. The buffalo must have enjoyed the juice from heaven, and when it stopped, it was probably like, "Now what?"

And when Phil collapsed, it just turned around and walked away in peace.

We still had a week to go on this trip, and Phil was the closest person to me. When I was reading, he was sitting next to me. When I was cooking, he was right there next to me, helping with the preparation of meals. When I had to answer the call of nature, I would have to say, with a pleasant smile on my face, "Hey buddy, I gotta do this alone."

Please, on your next safari, try not to be a Phil.

Chapter 3
The Story Within a Story

The time is six forty-five p.m., exactly fifteen minutes before dinner. We are at Spitzkoppe community bush camp in Namibia, just a little over eighty kilometres off the coast of the Atlantic Ocean. All seventeen clients have just returned from a forty-five minutes' walk to and from the Bushman paintings; a national heritage site that has been one of my favourites for many, many years. I love this campsite because we are far away from the city noises and lights. The nearest big town being Swakopmund, a coastal town popular for dolphin cruises, sky-diving, and quadbike tours on the dunes of the Namib Desert. We just spent two nights there and are done with towns, for now.

At this camp, there are no flush toilets, only long-drop Blair toilets, no running water, so we have to rely on the water from the water tank on our bus. That is why even our meals here are simple; usually just stews and one type of starch. The activities here are quite simple; a walk to the paintings, a walk to the natural stone bridge, and for those who love rock climbing, the pointed rock outcrop, after which this camp is named, is excellent for that; otherwise, one could just find some shade, open a book, and read.

This is my favourite campsite for storytelling, especially at night, just after dinner, under the beautiful, eye-catching stars of the African sky. My colleague and assistant, Mr Boombastic, wherever he got that name from, is throwing some final touches to our dinner, and from where I'm sitting, taking in the aroma, I'm pretty damn sure it is spaghetti bolognaise. That mouth-watering smell of melting cheese is unmistakable. A few girls are already setting the table while chatting away excitedly. I'm very much aware that everyone is eagerly waiting for my campfire stories.

The two days in Swakop were about activities and drinking and everyone doing their individual stuff, and now that we are back together again, the show must go on.

"Mr L." Someone calls out my name. It is the sweet young German girl, Tanya, that everyone loves. Her birthday is in three days in Etosha National Park. She is turning eighteen, and I can already see secret preparations from the other clients to throw her a surprise party. She just can't leave me alone, not that I hate it. She is so much fun to have around.

It's the way she speaks that tickles me; dragging out the

letter *L* when she says Mr L. She is in the bus close to the back seat.

Half turning in my seat, I respond, "Yes, my dear."

"I can't find my shoooes!" she says, in almost a whimper.

I respond again, "Where did you put them?"

"I don't knowwww!"

"So how do you expect me to know where they are if you yourself don't know where you put them?" I say with a light laugh. Some of the clients sitting with me by the fire also laugh.

"I don't knowwww!" she says, and at that moment everybody just bursts out laughing.

Then a few moments later, she is like, "Mr L," again.

I'm like, "Yes, dear."

"I found them," she says, walking up to me and taking a seat next to me.

"Where were they?"

And she is like, "Under the seat, in front of my seat in the bus."

We all laugh again, she laughs too.

In case you are wondering where that Mr L name came from. On the first day of our tour in Cape Town, Mr Bombastic introduced himself as Mr Boombastic and Tanya had said, "So Lesley, if he is Mr Bombastic, then who are you?" Mr Bombastic then said, "He is Mr L." From then on, she calls me by that name.

I see Mr Boombastic approaching the fireplace, rubbing his hands together. This can only mean one thing, he wants to announce dinner. Everybody realises this and instantly stops talking. We are all hungry, and Mr Bombastic is an excellent cook. We all love his cooking.

"Good evening, guys," he says, looking around to make sure

everybody is here. There is always that happy smile on his face. We all love him. He knows the right things to say at the right time, all the time. I envy him and sometimes can't help but wish I had his gift.

"Evening, Mr Boombastic," we all say in unison. We love doing this, and it always gives us a good laugh.

"Dinner is served," he says; that cool smile never leaving his face. "Tonight we have spaghetti bolognaise. Please enjoy, and please, ladies first."

There is a momentary *hu-hu* from all the ladies as they all rise to their feet and approach the table. The boys don't seem impressed.

Dinner plates are filled up, seats are taken, and our hands and mouths get busy. It's the perfect time to talk about tomorrow. It's a short briefing, I'm sure I will be done by the time the first person goes for second helpings. As I predicted, I'm done in eight minutes. Thirty minutes later, we are all done with dinner. Dishes take twenty minutes to do, and after that, everyone is back by the fire. My favourite client is next to me, checking something on her cell phone. I know we haven't got any signal here, but I tease her all the same.

"You on Snapchat?" I say, glancing at the cell phone in her hand.

She looks at me, smiles warmly, and puts the phone away, but not before teasing me back.

"Yes, reception here is the best. We should stay here two nights," we all laugh. Then, as if that was my cue, I lean forward in my chair and let loose.

"Well," I begin, everyone stops talking, except for Emily. In my village, they would refer to her as the twenty-four-hour radio station; someone who is always talking that even a fly can't land on their lips. She suddenly notices everyone is looking at her, shakes her shoulders, and utters an apology.

"Oh, I'm sorry. Didn't realise."

"A couple of years ago," I carry on, "we came here and camped on the other side of that mountain, over by the entry to the bushman's paintings, where you guys went this noon. No one is allowed to camp there any more coz visitors complained that they felt uncomfortable walking through someone else's campsite on their way to the paintings.

"Just like you guys tonight, almost everyone was gonna sleep outside. Very few tents were pitched. Mattresses were on the dry river bed there, and some guys had walked all the way here for sunset up by those rocks, and the stone bridge." I pause for a moment, sip on my favourite drink, gin and tonic, and proceed.

"In those days I did not have a bus driver's license, so I was just the tour leader and cook. So while everyone else was doing whatever they were doing, I was busy cooking. I had a big cast iron pot with a beef stew on the fire. Now you guys saw the big boulders just by the foot of the rocky hill with the climbing chain you used to climb up to the top?"

"Yeah, yeah," a few of them respond.

"The fireplace was just in front of those boulders, and I was stirring my pot, with my back to the boulders, in a slightly bent over position. On the other side of the fire by the bus were two Australian couples that had chosen to just sit by the fire and chat, even though it was still probably about an hour before sunset. I didn't mind them. So, I'm busy stirring my pot when one of the two guys, can't remember his name, suddenly says, "Ey, Lez."

I look up, and I'm like, "Yeah."

And he says, "What kinda cat is that?"

I look over my shoulder and almost leap across the fire. The couples, upon seeing my reaction, jump to their feet and make for the bus, all four of them fitting through the bus passenger side door like they were little beings. The beautifully spotted cat was in some sort of a crouched position less than six metres away from me. I avoided eye contact, backed away from it and stopped by the bus door. It stared at me for what seemed like a good three minutes before it got up, swung around, and disappeared behind the big rocks. It was limping noticeably.

The couples came out of the bus and stood next to me. Then one of the ladies said, "That's no ordinary cat, is it?"

Without taking my eyes off the big rocks, I said, "Nope, that's a leopard."

"Oh shit," one of my clients from across the fire says. There is total silence now, and I'm sure I can hear some whispering among them.

A young Australian guy, who likes to swear a lot, asks, "What was it gonna do?"

"I don't know, probably come give me a handshake," I say this with a soft chuckle.

All of a sudden, everyone seems scared. Tanya says, in a serious tone, "Are they that dangerous?" This is the first time she says something to me without saying my name first, and this tells me she is also scared.

"Not always," I answer her, "they don't usually attack people unless it's really necessary, usually coz they are territorial animals. They would rather avoid confrontation where possible. You see, leopards are very secretive animals. You can actually live with one for thirty years without knowing it. Coming out at night when everyone is asleep and going back to its hiding place before sunrise. The only evidence that there is one around would be the occasional disappearance of a goat or a dog."

"But this one seemed to be stalking you. Why was that?" she says.

"She was wounded, which makes her very dangerous because hunting becomes difficult for her."

"How do you know it was a she?" Another guy asks.

"Well," I respond, "I didn't see any balls hanging from under her tail." I laugh.

Then the guy sitting three chairs from me to my right, lighting a cigarette, speaks for the first time since dinner.

"So there are leopards here?"

I'm like, "Yeah, well, they are everywhere, we just don't see them. Look, I have been coming here for the last ten years, and that's the only leopard I have seen."

A Dutch lady in her mid-thirties asks, "Why did you avoid eye contact?"

I answer her, "Because if you stare at a leopard, unlike lions, they feel threatened. To them, it's a challenge, meaning you're planning something, and where they have no avenue for escape, attacking is the only way out. For example, if we were sitting under some tree and I looked up and saw a leopard, I would not tell you. I would just lure you away from the tree, and when we're a safe distance away, I would show you the leopard."

"That's interesting," Tanya says.

One client, a British lady, says, "So what happened after?"

"Nothing," I say, "I went back to my cooking, the couples went back inside the bus and sat in there until the rest of the group got back from sunset," I say this with a bit of a laugh.

At that moment, Michael, a young Australian, rises and goes to the bus, where he opens the side lockers and starts pulling at things.

"What you doing, Mike?" I ask him.

"I'm looking for me tent?" he says.

Jimmy, a British young man, says to Michael, "What the hell for, man?"

"I ain't sleeping outside no more, mate, not with leopards around. I didn't come to Africa to die," he says as he carries the tent to a clearing in the grass and starts pitching it.

"You such a sissy," Jimmy says as he gets up to go and help him with the tent.

"Call me what you like, but I'm sleeping in this tent. Who knows, could be lions up in here too and Lesley just ain't telling us. Why do you think dude sleeps up on the roof instead of down here with the rest of us? Wise up."

Oh my God, I can't stop laughing right now. Suddenly, they are all talking. Suddenly everyone is pitching tents, and some of them ask if they can join me up on the roof. No one is going to sleep outside tonight. I have killed it with my story. I get to my feet, stretch, and say, a reassuring smile on my face.

"All right guys, I'm sorry I scared you, but if it makes you feel better, I'm sleeping down here with you tonight. Those who would like to go on the roof of the bus, feel free to do so, but please do not sleepwalk."

We all laugh. I grab my mattress from the mattress compartment, lay it a few feet from the fire, grab my sleeping bag from my locker, and sit down on the mattress for a while, chatting a bit more with the few that will sleep outside with me. When we finally enter our sleeping bags, it doesn't take long for the snoring to begin.

"Good night, yah all," I say softly. Two or three respond. Today was one day, tomorrow is another.

Chapter 4
A Human Story

Tonight is a beautiful night. There is not a single cloud in the African skies; the skies painted by millions of brilliant stars. Two constellations are quite visible, Orion's belt on one side, the southern cross on the other, sitting just above the south-western horizon. We are camped at Madusa Camp, right on the demarcation line between Herero and Damaraland. Dinner, as usual, was great, barbequed snoek, roasted yellow corn on the cob, baked potatoes, garlic bread, plus a green salad on the side. A reasonably big fire in the middle is keeping us warm tonight. A few clients are in their tents already, some of them still quietly chatting, while some are already in dreamland, but there are still around ten sitting with me by the fire. Since this is home to the desert elephant, I am thinking of giving them a little talk on them. But before I open my mouth, Emily, the tall, slim blond from England, breaks the silence.

"So Lez, how about an animal less story."

"Animal less story?" I ask as I pick up my coffee mug and take a long sip."

"Yeah, you know, a human story. One without wild animals." She is smiling at me the way a kid who thinks she has put you in a corner smiles.

A few other clients nod in agreement.

"Yeah, Lez," a nineteen-year-old Australian boy interjects. "Maybe the day you will never forget, or," he pauses for a moment, searching for words, "the most embarrassing day of your life."

"Well," I say, closing my eyes and searching my brain's archives for a human story. Then, when I stumble upon one, everyone is silent. "A human story," I give out a short chuckle before continuing. "I ain't never heard of such. But anyways, one day I and my colleague, Tich, were driving from Windhoek to Cape Town after finishing a fifteen-day tour of Namibia. We call it just a transit. We had started off around midday and covered about 500 kilometres when I decided to pull into a filling station in Keetmanshoop for toilets and a cup of coffee or something. It was around eight p.m. Since this was a long drive, a little over a thousand four hundred kilometres, I was happy both of us could drive. We took turns driving the overland truck. If he was driving, I was sleeping, and if I was driving, he was sleeping in the aisle at the back. Occasionally, if needed, we would talk through the communication hatch between the cab and the bus section of the truck.

We still had three hundred kilometres to go to the Vioolsdrif border, and the only other town between Keetmanshoop and the border, Grunau, would be closed by the time we got there, so this was the best place to briefly stop for coffee, snacks, a leg stretch, and bathrooms.

After switching off the truck, I told Tich through the hatch that this was a pee stop, to which he said, he was okay for now, so I could go on ahead without him. I first went into the toilet before going into the small convenience store. In about six minutes, I was back in the truck and ready to go again. The coffee, Red Bull, and snacks kept me so energised that I didn't even feel the 300 kilometres to the border. I didn't even stop in Grunau, I just drove straight through and only stopped in the parking lot at Vioolsdrif. Through the hatch again, I told Tich we were at the border. I reminded him to lock the back door and proceeded to immigration.

After filling out the border form and telling the official that we were only two, he asked, "Where's the other one?"

I told him he was coming, took a bit longer because he was sleeping in the back when we arrived. The official stamped my passport, gate pass, and handed them to me. I walked out and went back to the truck. When I tried the back door, it was locked, so I got into the cab and called out through the hatch. There was no response. I swung around in my seat and peeped through the hatch; all I could see was a sleeping bag, no sign of Tich. Without getting alarmed, and not wanting to entertain the disturbing thought in the back of my mind, I jumped out of the cab, rushed to the bathrooms, and checked, still no sign of Tich. Then suddenly, without wanting to accept it, I knew what had happened.

"Oh, my Gawd," One of the clients from across the fire, says with an audible sigh.

"Yeah," I respond, "I had left him three hundred kilometres back in Keetsmans."

There is a murmur among the clients as they take this all in.

"Dude later decided to go to the toilet after all. Assuming he was sleeping in the back, I had driven off. All his stuff was with me, I mean, his small backpack with his passport and other documents, wallet, and cell phone were in the truck, so he had not been able to call me or our twenty-four-hour emergency call number."

"So what did you do?" Emily says, panic in her voice.

"There is 300 kilometres between us now, about five-six hours drive at least, given that it's late at night. It's after midnight, there is not a lot of traffic on the highway until maybe around six in the morning, which means the chances of him getting a lift are close to zero. So I went back to immigration and explained the situation to the official who had served me before.

"I called my ops manager and told him the story. He understood and advised me to see if immigration could assist in any way. Since this was a twenty-four-hour border, I kindly asked if I could leave Tich's passport and wallet with them, so that whatever time he would arrive, he would be assisted. They said yes. The ops manager said he would call one of the lodges we frequently used on our tours to ask them to send someone to the filling station and try to find Tich, and maybe let him stay till morning when he would be able to hitchhike. I could not wait for him coz the truck I was driving was needed in Cape Town by midday.

"I crossed into South Africa, still unable to accept what had just happened. 677 kilometres more for me to do, alone, was unimaginably not so cool; but then, I guess that was way better than being stuck at a filling station in a foreign country, with no cash, no documents, unable to hitchhike coz no one would believe your story. A few minutes into South Africa, as I unhappily glanced at the Cape Town 600 kilometres sign on the side of the N7 highway, the ops manager called me and told me the good news. One of the lodges had sent a driver to find Tich, and he was now safely in one of their rooms. I smiled as I hung up and pushed my foot down on the accelerating pedal."

"Damn!" One of the clients says, "That wasn't cool."

"I know," I respond. "Well," I get to my feet, stretch, and tell them I am off to bed.

I leave them thinking about the story, and as I pull my sleeping bag over my face, I hear one of them say, "What a human story."

Silently, I say, you ain't heard nothing yet, I am as good with human stories as I am with animal ones. Good night.

Chapter 5
My Hand Is Stuck!

"So, Lez," the young bloke from New Zealand said when I was just about to say good night, "you ain't got no other stories besides the lion ones?"

"What stories do you wanna hear?" I said, settling back in my chair. I had prayed that no one would request a story from me tonight. I just wanted to go to bed before midnight. Tomorrow would be an early start for us and the 320 kilometres waiting to be done was no joke. I checked my watch; the time was eight forty-five p.m. I could do another forty to sixty minutes.

"I don't know," he said, "maybe an elephant, hyena, hippo,

or any other interesting stories."

I cleared my throat and thought for a second; then I said, "Well, a few years ago, I was gonna catch an early morning bus to Victoria Falls to prepare for a Vic to Cape trip that I was starting in five days." I paused for a moment, then decided, this wasn't the story for tonight. I had to think fast.

Then I smiled when I found the story I was looking for tucked away in the archives of my mind. A story that even I find hard to believe. A story a grade seven classmate of mine had shared with us many years back. "Two marijuana traders crossed the Zambezi River from Zambia into Zimbabwe in the early hours of the day," I began, "they could not use the Kariba-Siavonga border because marijuana was very illegal those days. Because they couldn't find somewhere shallow enough for them to cross below the dam wall, they had to walk ten kilometres downstream before they could cross; which made their journey much longer than it was supposed to be. Once on the Zim side, they had to find food as soon as possible, or they would collapse from hunger. From the river to the beginning of Nyamhunga township, where they could get food, it's about twenty-five kilometres of thick forest and is also a game reserve with potentially dangerous animals; but these guys had lived in Kariba, where these animals are a common thing, all their life, they weren't worried about that, it was the hunger they dreaded the most."

There was total silence around the campfire at Twyfelfontein Camp. All twenty-two clients were sitting with me around the fire. On arrival from Spitzkoppe, they had all chosen to get beers and other drinks from the bar and bring them to the fire. This was also to avoid having to walk back from the bar in the dark, drunk, and risk walking into desert elephants that had been spotted nearby just before sunset.

"Ey, Lez," one of the clients had asked me early on, "you say desert elephants are more temperamental than the other elephants, why is that?"

"Well," I had told him, "since these guys live in the desert, where water is very scarce, they have to walk long distances before they can find it; this makes them very angry and usually aggressive. Just like a hungry man being an angry man, a thirsty elephant is an angry elephant."

"I see," he had nodded, before continuing to pitch his tent.

Back to the marijuana boys.

"After walking for about two hours up and down hills, occasionally stopping to rest under big trees, they struck it lucky. A dead rhino lay beside a big patch of acacia bushes. They looked at each other momentarily and smiled happily. How they concluded that the rhino was dead, I have no idea but I would like to think that it looked dead. This was mana from heaven, right there. Meat on a silver plate, and I'm talking tones of it; over 1.5 tons of meat." I paused and couldn't help chuckling with the rest of the group as they started to assume where the story was going.

They were wrong.

"Now," I proceeded when the laughing subsided, "wild animals, especially rhinos, have an acute sense of hearing and smell. Their eyesight is bad, so in compensation, nature gave them excellent hearing and smell, such that you could never walk up to them without being detected unless you are downwind from them and extremely quiet."

"Interesting," Tamia, the quietest of them all, spoke for the first time since we finished dinner.

"Rhinos are part of the Big Five, aren't they?"

"Yes, they are," I answered her, but felt the need to explain a bit more. "You see, rhinos can be very dangerous, they are huge, have sharp deadly horns that can drill a hole through you quite easily, but they aren't as aggressive as they are often made out to be. Having had several encounters with them during walks, I have concluded that, more often than not, they either hear or smell you before they see you, and they react by just bolting in any direction, which could be where you are. Many a time, a rhino has had to brake just a few metres from me, turn, and scurry off in the opposite direction because it only saw me when it was very close. Now imagine a situation where it doesn't see you at all, wouldn't it just run you over?"

There were silent murmurs of agreement.

"So," I continued, "the rhino wasn't moving, it didn't seem like it was breathing; the one eye that they could see was lifelessly open and white. Its rectum had slipped outside the open end of its digestive tract, a condition known as rectal prolapse, and this alone could have convinced the guys that the rhino was dead. They had matches, but they didn't have a knife with which to cut the meat, so one of them climbed up on top of a nearby hill to see if they were anywhere near a village of some sort; they weren't. In the distance, about five or so kilometres, gleaming objects caught his eye, and suddenly he knew what he was looking at. It was Barotseland, a huge dumping area close to the Kariba-Harare Highway. He knew if he ran there, he would find some sort of sharp object or piece of iron sheet that they could use as a knife. After giving a thumbs-up sign to his friend, he broke into a run towards the dumping site."

"Excuse me, guys," Mohanis, our driver, who had heard this story several times before, called out from the bus door, "does anyone still need anything from the bus? I'm about to lock it and go to bed, got a long drive tomorrow."

"No, we good." The clients answered in unison. "Good night, Mohanis!"

I chuckled. They sometimes sounded like school kids, but we loved it. It always sent us to bed with a smile on our faces.

"What had seemed like a short distance to the dumpsite turned out to be much longer than expected," I continued with the story. "After about an hour, the guy who had stayed behind, watching over the rhino, grew impatient. His hunger was suddenly unbearable. There was only one thing he could do; push his hand through the rhino's anus and find soft organs like the liver and the lungs. If he managed to rip them out, by the time his friend got back, they would be roasting on the fire."

There was a loud chuckle from the clients.

I laughed out loud too, rising to my feet because this part needed me to demonstrate with my whole body for a better understanding.

"So without hesitating, the guy pushed his hand into the rhino's backside, through the rectum, all the way up to his elbow, and started groping around. This must have tickled the rhino, which suddenly woke up, its whole body shaking violently, and leaped to its feet."

I paused for a moment while they all laughed.

Some guests camping next to us, who had been following the story, couldn't hold back their laughter as well. Before the laughing subsided totally, I continued, "The rhino did not take time to investigate the cause of its internal discomfort, it just knew it had to get away. Whatever was stuck in its backside had to be shaken off somehow, and the best way would be to run as fast as possible through the bushes. So it ran. The guy, on the other hand, could not pull his hand out coz upon waking up, the muscles around the rhino's anus had tightened in an attempt to suck the rectum back in, resulting in making it impossible to free himself. So, as he was dragged around in the forest, he started yelling, "The animal is getting awaaaaaaay!"

His friend, who apparently was now near, heard the yelling and responded by yelling back, "Let it get awaaaay!"

Then the guy yelled, "How can I let it get away when I've got my hand stuck in its backside!"

"Hold onto a treeee or somethin!"

"How do I hold onto a tree when the animal is running so faaaast!"

Oh my God, now there was a chorus of laughter, best time for me to disappear without anyone noticing, or I would be coaxed into telling another story. I surreptitiously slid around the bus and tiptoed to my tent, got inside, and zipped up.

I could still hear them laughing long after I got into my sleeping bag.

The next day, as we drove to Etosha National Park, I told them what had caused the rhino to appear dead. Rhinos enjoy eating euphorbia plants, sucking on the poisonous milk latex they produce. Now, although the poison has no deadly effect on the rhinos, it intoxicates them to the point of motionlessness, where they sleep for hours without moving a limb. This rhino had helped himself to a lot of that drink.

"What happened to the guy eventually?" One client asked.

"His hand is still stuck, and the rhino is still running around trying to shake him off."

We all chuckled as we drove through Henderson's gate of Etosha. The real game drive had begun. Everyone went for their cameras as I said, "Welcome to Etoshaaa!"

Goodnight, oh, or is it good morning or good afternoon, wherever you are reading this from?

Keep smiling!

Chapter 6
Where the Maned Brothers Rest

Having driven just over a thousand kilometres through one of Africa's mighty deserts, the Kalahari Desert, alone, without resting, my body was almost giving up. My eyes felt heavy, my arms stiff, and my neck was a bit sore. The memories of my just-ended twenty-day tour of Namibia had kept me going despite the tiredness; the coast, the national heritage sights, and the cultural visits had been more than amazing, they had been exceptional. Looking out either side of the highway now, seeing nothing but the open plains, stretching well into the horizon, everything changed. Not taking anything away from Botswana, and not saying the country has nothing to offer either, I mean, it surely has the Okavango Delta, the famous Savuti National Park, the Chobe National Park, but these were nowhere near where I was driving, except, of course, for Makgadikgadi Pan, which lay on my right. But I had done enough sight-seeing for now. I just wanted to get home and be with my family and friends and share my experiences with them, watching their eyes widen as I would be doing what I was best at, telling stories like no other person they knew.

I had to stop and rest. My first and last stop since departing Windhoek, Namibia's capital city, had been at the Trans Kalahari border, and because it had not been busy at all. In less than thirty minutes I was done with all border formalities and back at the wheel, happily inhaling the welcoming, cool, fresh air of the Botswana side of the Kalahari Desert. I clearly remember swearing loudly as I shifted into the last gear of my 4x4 on realising I had not, as planned, made use of the toilets there, but then again, those toilets are usually not very hospitable, I am sure you catch my drift. The bush or roadside was a better option, and up until now I had managed to not pay attention to my bladder's distress calls; but now, I had to go. It was now tormenting me, and I knew the last fifty kilometres to my intended place of stay for the night would not be doable, so, without giving it much thought, I steered off-road and stopped by what had once been a nice picnic spot.

The big acacia tree that had provided shade there had given

in to old age. All that remained of it was just a small portion of the almost fully decomposed trunk and pieces of bark that had fallen victim to the ever-harvesting termites of the Kalahari Desert.

I switched off the car, stepped out slowly as I listened to my aching body, and stretched while I yawned and scanned the area around me for any unwanted company, there was none. I looked up at the clear blue sky and nodded, murmuring the words, "It sure is a beautiful day." I checked my watch, it was five p.m. and beginning to cool down as it would only be a few hours before the sun disappeared, perfect time for the kings and queens of the jungle to get ready to go hunting. Wait a minute. Did I just say kings of the jungle? Do not get all excited now, this story has nothing to do with those lazy guys who spend three-quarters of their day lying under trees and bushes, occasionally rolling onto their backs, and the males sometimes doing something as silly as squirting urine into the air. Besides, there were no big trees in sight, not even bushes big enough to accommodate these giant cats, well, except for one bush about sixty metres from the main road to my left. The grass was not very tall, such that if anything, even the size of a leopard was to move through it, it would be noticeable, so I walked about twenty metres away from the car along the main road and began to set my bladder free, enjoying the moment with closed eyes and a distant smile about my face. There was total silence except for the soft trickling sound of my urine as it came into contact with the grass in front of me. When done, I did what men always do, shake shake shake and retrieve before pulling on my trouser zipper; then it happened. The hair at the back of my head stood on end.

Okay, now that I am pretty sure that I got your attention, I am going to get right into it, but before that, I have got to say something. There are only two things in Africa—no, actually, three—that can cause your hair to stand on end, number one, the most feared, most deadly, and most venomous snake in the world, the notorious black mamba, number two, the mighty king of the jungle, the lion, and number three, the thought that a ghost is staring at you from the shadows at night while walking through a graveyard. It was not night yet, and I was not driving through a graveyard, so that ruled out the ghosts. It was in the desert with no rocky hills, caves, and large trees, so that ruled out the notorious guy, leaving us with only one culprit, I guess we all know who that is.

    Slowly, I turned around and found myself staring right into the menacing, expressionless eyes of a male lion, frozen, less than ten metres away from me. Right between me and my car. There was nowhere to go. The most feared animal in Africa was staring up at me with such intensity I almost asked it if there was something I could do for it. My knees felt like jelly as I weighed my options. Run? How, on jelly legs? Fight? How, without a weapon. I weigh around 100 kg and a full-grown male lion, between 200 and 250 kg. And, having been a safari guide for more than ten years, I knew exactly what I was up against, and all the things I had said during my briefings before walks and drives in game reserves like Kruger National Park, Hwange National Park, and Mana Pools, started coming back. I realised this day that, remaining still and staring a lion down is not as easy as presumed, it is not even voluntary, it is because one cannot do anything else. You cannot move as fear grips you so tight that your body can not react to the commands coming from your brain, and it is amazing how we all suddenly turn Christian, praying to a God whose existence we did not even acknowledge before.

Back to the maned brother, he seemed very calm and collected as he continued to stare at me, his tail swishing slowly from side to side, a sign that he still was undecided on what to do next. I thought of turning tail but then realised I could not move my legs, and even if I could, outrunning a lion seemed just as difficult as engaging in a fight against it. My many years of being a safari guide had taught me that never turn your back on a cat, as that would be a sign of fear or weakness and would result in actually getting attacked.

Suddenly, I remembered my grandmother, many years back in the village where I grew up, calming and luring a dog by getting down on one knee and tapping at the ground with her fingers while whistling softly. Instinctively, I dropped down on one knee and started doing that. Surprisingly, the tail swishing stopped, and the lion sat down on its hind legs, then eventually lay on its tummy. For a second, his eyes left me and went over to that bush about sixty or so metres away from us, but I did not follow them. I knew that instant that he was not alone, and that realisation alone sent shivers throughout my body. Squaring off with one lion was one thing, but being surrounded by a pride was unthinkably catastrophic.

Then, as I was wondering what would happen if the lion suddenly came over and sat or stood beside me, I heard the sound of an approaching vehicle from behind me. I chose not to turn around and look. A few moments later, a small open truck pulled up about twenty metres opposite us, and through the corner of my eye, I could see the shock in the eyes of the old man driving it.

Without saying anything, he killed the engine and opened the passenger side door, cautiously stepping out onto the road, his eyes not leaving us for a second. He cautiously went to the back of the vehicle. The lion's gaze, which had left me momentarily, followed the guy around as he lifted what seemed like a blanket covering something. His hand reached under it and came out with a huge chunk of what looked like donkey or horse meat. He threw it a few metres away from the back of his car, after which he climbed back into his vehicle. The lion, who immediately smelled the fresh meat, suddenly rose to its feet, and quickly trotted over to the meat, and started tearing at it. As I turned around, I noticed another male lion trotting from the bush towards me. I told myself that that was the end of me, but miraculously, as if I did not even exist, he ran a few metres past me and joined the brother. Slowly and cautiously, I rose and tiptoed to my car, opened the door, and slid in. I quickly closed the door, lowered my head onto the steering wheel, and listened to my loudly racing heart.

My saviour looked across at me and said, "Do you believe in God?"

I said, "I don't know, man."

Then, with a slight shake of his head, he murmured, "You should." Without saying another word, he started his car and drove off. After watching the brothers feast on their gift from the stranger for nearly half an hour, I started my car and continued with my journey. Instead of pulling into my initially intended place of stay for the night, I suddenly had enough energy to drive another 350 kilometres, and, as I laid my head down on the soft pillow in my hotel room later that night, I remember being so grateful that I had lived to see another day.

Chapter 7
Did This Happen?

"Yo, Lez," the youngest client on my tour, spoke from across the fire. His name was Jim.

"Yap," I said.

"Do you got a story for us tonight or you've told us all you got?" He chuckled as he moved the wood around in the fire to get it going. It wasn't a cold night, but that didn't matter; a fire is like a tradition to us campers. We just love it. We even call it the African TV. On a camping tour, that's where interesting stories are shared, marshmallows are baked, and even bonding is done.

There were twelve clients by the fire with me. To me, that's a good number for a story, but tonight, since I had driven 750 kilometres through the Namib Desert, on mostly gravel roads, I was a bit tired and just wanted to listen to others talk. If my colleague hadn't gone to bed immediately after dinner, I would have gone to bed already, but at this campsite, the crew had to go to bed last, as the area was vulnerable to wildfires. Since it was the dry season, we had to make sure the fire was totally put out, something you couldn't trust clients to execute properly, especially after a glass or two of red wine, gin and tonic, and a couple of Windhoek lagers.

It was at this bush campsite where, a few months back, because we use bush toilets (which are just a hole in the ground or a small clearing), one crew member had gone to answer the call of nature, tried to burn the toilet paper she had used, and almost razed the whole campsite to the ground. Luckily for them, it had been a windless night, and putting out the fire had not been that difficult.

So, since I was going to be the last one to leave the fireplace, one good story was going to be doable; one good lion story to send them all off to bed by midnight.

"I got too many stories to ever run out," I chuckled, took a sip of my coffee, and cleared my throat. A couple of hands clapped, and a few that were standing, watching the glittering stars of the African sky, took their seats and waited.

Jim opened his fifth beer and said, "We're all ears."

"Well," I began, "I was gonna tell you a story about a guy who saved a lion from a pack of wild dogs without even a single weapon, but nope, I don't want some of you having nightmares."

They all laughed and agreed with me.

"A couple of years ago, I was driving up to the north, on a rescue mission with the company's mechanic. Apparently one of our overland trucks had gotten stuck in a river bed, and in trying to force it out, the driver had burnt out the clutch.

Driving down this steep hill just twenty kilometres out of Kamanjab, a little Himba town in Kaokoland, with Edward, the mechanic, snoring in the passenger seat, I saw a cloud of dust about three hundred metres ahead of me beside the main road. At first, I thought they were bulls fighting, as there were a few cattle scattered around in the area, most of which had stopped grazing and were also intently watching the cloud of dust.

I pulled over on the side of the road and shook Edward's shoulder. He woke up and stared at me. "What's up?" he said while rubbing his eyes with the back of both his hands.

"Look over there," I said, pointing in the direction of the dust, which was beginning to settle down, exposing a Toyota 4x4 twin cab that lay on its roof. "That's an accident."

I quickly opened my door and jumped out, my cell phone in hand. Edward, who was now wide awake and seemingly scared, followed suit. From the skid marks on the tarred road, the driver must have lost control right from the top of the hill and ended up rolling the vehicle three to four times towards the right side of the road, flattening a couple of acacia bushes and grass in the process. With Edward beside me, we started cautiously towards the car.

Then my heart skipped a bit. Two young ladies, covered in red dust, emerged from the bushes by the car, dusting themselves off with their palms. We stopped and then saw a guy lying unconscious on the ground on our side of the car. They must have all been thrown out the broken windows as the car rolled.

We were about fifty yards from them and didn't want to alarm them. Just after an accident, victims are usually so scared and fragile that they don't trust anyone. Sometimes they fear those that may try to take advantage by stealing from them, so one has to be very careful, especially where the victims are Europeans and the rescuers are Africans, in Africa. I looked around for any shoes that may have come off anyone coz, apparently, at an accident, if shoes come off, someone is dead, a certain European firefighter had once told me on tour. "Shoes don't just come off," he had said.

I wasn't sure how many passengers had been in the 4x4 so I started looking around for any more people. The young ladies had noticed us and were now chatting quietly by their friend, who hadn't moved. One of them walked over to a Samsonite bag lying open on the ground and pulled out a greyish blanket. She walked back to her friend and placed the blanket over the unconscious guy, covering him up the way we cover up a dead body.

That is when I approached them.

"Hi guys, my name is Lesley, this is Edward, my colleague, we're first aiders. Anything we can do to help?"

They both just stared at us and started sobbing.

"First we need to call you an ambulance," I said as I searched my phone for the number, "then we need to call the vehicle owner." With those roof tents on it, it was obviously one of those self-drive vehicles for hire.

The girls hugged each other and continued to sob. Then the unexpected happened.

The unconscious guy suddenly pushed the blanket covering him aside and sat up. After saying this, I paused, remembering how it had happened, I couldn't help laughing. Most of the clients laughed with me. I'm sure they already could see what was coming next. We laughed for a good two minutes, occasionally stopping to gather up some more energy.

"We all turned to look at him," I continued, "and when he started to get up, all hell broke loose. The two girls momentarily looked at each other, their eyes wide with terror, and took off in the direction of the forest further down the highway, Edward following behind them like Ben Johnson himself." The loud laughter from the clients made me stop again. I used this opportunity to hurry into the bus for my bottle of beer. When I came back to the fireplace, the laughing had subsided a bit.

"I have to be very honest with you here, guys," I said, "I don't think it was courage that kept me from running as well. I think I had frozen. We Africans are scared of dead people too, and to see one actually coming back to life is no laughing matter. I just couldn't move. I watched in horror as the guy finally got to his feet and got his balance. His whole body was covered in dust which made him look like a real ghost. He looked at me, looked in the direction where Edward and the girls had run, slowly shook his head, and staggered to the flipped 4x4, where, with his back against the side of the car, he slid down to the ground and just sat there, panting.

"I was now fully recovered from the shock. I walked slowly up to him and knelt on one knee in front of him. His half-open eyes searching for mine, he reached out his right hand, laid it on my shoulder, and spoke softly, his voice almost a faint whisper."

"What the hell happened?"

"You had an accident," I replied, my voice matching his. "Help is on the way. I am a first aider. Please remain still. Are you feeling any pain anywhere, your back, your neck?"

He shook his head and looked away from me. Then he spoke again, "And the girls, I saw them running. Are they okay?"

I nodded and told him to stay put while I went to look for them. I couldn't tell him why they had bolted. I got up, went round to the other side of the Toyota, and called an ambulance.

When I was done calling, I saw the girls slowly walking back. Edward was nowhere to be seen. They went straight to him and knelt beside him. They spoke in German, but I could sense the anger in his voice. I'm sure he wasn't impressed to hear they had run away from him coz they thought he was a ghost. It took a while before they managed to calm him down and finally embrace each other. I called the vehicle owner, explained everything, and gave him the coordinates of the accident scene. Ten minutes later, as an ambulance from Kamanjab pulled up beside my car, Edward returned, and I couldn't stop laughing at him as we proceeded to our destination, which was still a good 300 kilometres away."

"Man," I teased him. "What are you doing here? You should be in the Olympics, dude. Damn, you faster than two Ben

Johnsons!"

"Shut up!" he said, giving me a friendly smack on the shoulder. I couldn't stop laughing, I just couldn't. I could still visualise his arms swinging back and forth with the speed of pistons as he ran for dear life back there.

We said good night, and after putting out the fire, I climbed onto the roof of the bus, and within a few minutes, I was in dreamland under the shining stars of the African sky, the southern cross clearly showing off just above the rocky outcrop to my right.

Chapter 8
Wildlife Horror

WHEN THE LIONS VISIT

Having completed the first part of our two weeks training as recruits for one of the biggest tour companies in the world, we were ready to proceed to the next level, the practical side of

Overland guiding. The whole first week had been consumed by mostly theory, stuff like learning company policies and accounts, meals, and trip planning, plus client handling; not so exciting but very important and necessary. All six of us, three white South Africans, two of us black Zimbabweans, and Jerry, a black South African, could not wait to leave the city of Johannesburg. We were ready for the bush; ready for boot camp; so, leaving Johannesburg early in the morning, we headed for Balule Game Reserve, home to the Big Five and part of the Greater Kruger National Park.

Now, I know some of you are already wondering, what's the Big Five? Well, let me tell you. The Big Five are the five wild animals that gave hunters a tough time during hunts for trophies, the most feared and potentially dangerous animals on land in Africa. And, please note, the name has absolutely nothing to do with size, weight, or looks. The hippo, the giraffe, and eland are much bigger and even heavier than some of the Big Five. And, statistically, hippos and crocodiles kill more people than most wild animals in Africa, but back in the day, nobody hunted them for trophies, hence their exclusion from the list. Nowadays, we even have the small five, and the ugly five, but let that be a story for another day.

That being clarified, let's get back to our story.

The long, tiring journey of about 500 kilometres took us the whole day to do in our strikingly beautiful overland truck, and on arrival, just before sunset, we offloaded our gear and set up camp, just 300 metres from the Main Lodge. Our HR manager, who had travelled with us, and would be part of the team training and evaluating us, was given a room in the lodge, and the rest of us stayed at the campsite. The campsite was in the form of a Boma, a circular roofless structure built of wooden poles fastened together by wooden trusses, nails, wire, and, in some places, rope. Picture an oversized cattle kraal with an entrance resembling that of a Blair toilet, the one with a hairpin turn. There is no door, but if you are inside, you cannot see outside, and if you are outside, you cannot see inside, meaning, animals such as cats and dogs can enter at will, you see where I am going?

"Guys, I suggest we pitch tents before dark," I said. And, to my surprise, all three white boys said no.

"We have a big fire burning all night and stretcher beds too, no need for tents," one of them said. His name was Henk, a long-haired Caucasian guy of Australian origin who had been with the company longer than any of us. He was here not as a trainee, but as the HR manager's assistant.

"But, guys," I insisted, pointing at the thick dark clouds over our heads, "what if it rains? Those are rain-bearing clouds up there."

"Ney, it ain't gonna rain, you just a coward, that's all." He laughed and carried on with whatever he was doing by the kitchen area.

Quietly, Jerry, the black South African guy, pitched his tent about fifteen metres to my left, and I decided to follow suit. I had to have somewhere to run should it rain. Besides, sleeping outside, no matter how beautiful the sky is, in a Big Five area is un-African. We do not dice with death. When my tent was up, I realised the entrance was not facing the campfire as it normally should, and wanted to swing it around then but decided I would do it later. Temperatures could have easily been around forty degrees Celsius and I badly needed a drink, a very cold one with alcohol in it. So just after placing my stretcher bed in front of my tent, I sat down on it, opened a cold beer, and sipped on it like a thirsty gold miner. Stive, my Zimbabwean colleague, walked up to me and placed his stretcher bed next to mine.

Sitting down on it, and smiling, he said, "I guess we can share one tent, nuh?"

"So long as you don't snore, man, don't want lions in my tent," I responded, with a smile as well.

"Well, finally, we're here. Thanx for hooking me up, bro." He half-turned towards me, still smiling, and extended his hand for a shake. I took it, nodded, and got to my feet.

"No worries, bro, we're good. Now let's get this dinner prepared," I said and walked over to the kitchen area, where we all started cutting vegetables, and in no time, dinner was cooking.

Round about seven p.m., we were all having dinner; a tasty butternut soup to start with, followed by roasted potatoes, rump steaks, a Greek salad, and tomato and onion sauce. The management team that had joined us for dinner was very impressed by the food, and as we ate, we shared all sorts of stories from politics, religion, business, to personal experiences in the tourism industry.

The big fire in the middle did not disappoint. The stars were amazing, with all the rain clouds now gone. But without the moon, the darkness was intense. The light bulb attached to a brunch of the big syringa tree by the kitchen illuminated the whole Boma. The setup here was fancy, with the light switch nailed to the trunk of the huge tree, two nice wooden tables by the sink, and a nice big wooden board leaning against the wooden fence with metal hooks where you could hang pots and pans to dry. I was already having ideas in my head as I took in every inch of the area, partially listening to the stories being shared.

Close to midnight, our HR manager checked his watch, glanced at the lodge manager, and nodded. It was time to call it a night. Together, they thanked us for the wonderful dinner and left for the lodge, one of the lodge guides leading the way, a 458 magnum held firmly in his hands.

Jerry got up too, said good night, and went to his tent. As he pulled down his tent's zipper, he said, out of the blue, "You guys ota be crazy sleeping outside like this?

Henk replied with a wave of his hand, and a chuckle, saying, "Wild animals, especially lions, have a special gift of smelling fear and cowardice. You being in the tent makes you the weakest and most scared one. Good luck tonight."

Jerry said no more. A few minutes later, he was snoring.

Now, I am an African who spent seven years of his young life in the village heading cattle and listening to scary tales of wild animal attacks, witchcraft, and ghost stories. This makes me highly superstitious. I have heard of sacred mountains, caves, rivers, and springs where people had disappeared or become disoriented for days, weeks, and months after having said certain things or done certain things deemed disrespectful. My father, who worked as a game ranger for over twenty years, had told me a story of some scouts who had been visited by lions just because they had mentioned them or wished to see them. That again, is a story for another day.

I was not going to sleep out here on some stretcher bed, come rain come thunder, but as I entertained these thoughts, the silence seemed to take over, and as I lay back on the stretcher, seeing that my Zimbabwean colleague had also done the same, the white boys on the other side of the fire suddenly quiet and one of them already in snore land. I vaguely remember seeing Henk, the long-haired guy getting up, and approaching the light switch on the tree trunk. I also remember him ignoring me when I told him to at least leave the light on. Unbeknownst to us, our worst nightmare was approaching.

At some time around two-thirty in the morning, I woke up with a start. The piercingly loud screaming, accompanied by scratching noises, coming from my left by Jerry's tent had woken me up, together with the rest of the other guys. No, it was coming from inside the tent, but because the night was pitch black, I could not see anything. The fear in Jerry's voice only meant one thing, lions were in his tent. Thinking fast, I reached down behind me and fumbled for the zipper of my tent so I could open the door and slide in, but it was nowhere to be found. Remember, I had intended to swing the tent around and bring the entrance to the front but had forgotten to do it.

Swearing softly, I gave up and grabbed hold of one of the tent poles supporting the tent and started shaking the whole tent vigorously to try and scare off any lion that might have spotted me. Of course, it was a desperate move, but remember, desperate moments call for desperate measures. I was not going to die without a fight. But, even as I write this story, I cannot help but laugh at myself. How the hell do you scare off a lion by shaking a tent? The guy would just be like, "Seriously?" There was also absolutely no way I was going around to the other side of the tent in that darkness, risking being noticed by the lions. In my mind, these were my last moments on earth. Without a weapon of some sort, very few men can stand a chance against a lion. The full-grown males weigh around 250 kg, so if he happens to knock you over and sit on you, there is no rising from there. All this I knew first hand as someone who had been guiding in big-game national parks for over ten years now.

I was just waiting to die, even though no one is ever prepared to die. The fear that grips you is immeasurable. It causes your heart to pound so loud you would think everyone nearby can hear it. Especially us Africans fear death, we do not dice with it. For example, when airplanes develop technical faults in mid-air, it is mostly us folks whom you hear screaming and praying loudly, reciting all the many verses in the bible. White people, on the other hand, are special, together with their cousins, the Asians. Big, dangerous things do not scare them easily, especially if they have never actually witnessed someone getting killed by them. That's why you hear many stories of them leaving their vehicles to go and try to grab a selfie with a lion. But, that also is a story for another day. Let's get back to the issue at hand.

Suddenly, something zipped past me, through the glowing coals from the dying fire. I did not see it, I just felt it. The wind it blew towards me felt like that from a jet engine. Whatever it was, it was fast and had not seen me. As my eyes began to adjust to the darkness, I saw something move across the fireplace from me. At first, it looked like a huge male lion, but then as the image got clearer, I realised it was the long-haired boy, Henk. He was holding a chair in his hands and blindly swinging it from side to side at the invisible lions. His long blond hair had made him look like a male lion and had prompted me to scream, "Lion!"

Because it was a warm night, we were all shirtless, we had on only boxer shorts, and my dark skin had prevented him from seeing me, and him being white, with a good shade of tan, had made him look like a lion itself. Instinctively, I shouted, "Switch on the light!"

It was only then that he saw me, since the chaos had begun. Obediently, he dropped the chair, rushed over to the tree trunk with the light switch, and hit it. Ironically, he is the same guy I had nicely asked to at least leave the lights on in case we got visitors, and he had rudely responded by saying, "Nothing ain't coming, Lesley, you just scared coz you're a coward."

Now here we were.

Now, let us take a break and think about this. When faced with death, we do not think about anything or anyone else but ourselves and our fate. For instance, I did not think about the three white boys, I did not for one second think about Stive, who had been lying in the now-empty stretcher bed a few feet from mine. This, however, taught me one terrifying thing, that, when we eventually die, we die alone, thinking only about ourselves and our fate. Scary stuff.

Anyway, the flooding light from the bulb hanging from the tree's branch lit up the whole Boma, and when we both looked around us, there were just the two of us standing. The second white guy, Tom, just sat there like a hypnotised someone, his hands clutching at his stomach and his eyes never leaving the fireplace in front of him. The third white guy, Richard, was nowhere to be seen, only his empty stretcher bed lay there. Steve was nowhere to be seen either, and for a moment it dawned on me that he also, like Richard, had been snatched by the lions. Jerry had suddenly stopped screaming, probably finally dead from the lions going at him this whole time. I remember frantically looking around me for the lions. There were none in sight, but that is not uncommon, they can snatch and disappear with the speed of a tiger.

While I was still trying to figure things out, I heard the sound of a zipper being pulled from Jerry's tent. I turned and looked over at the tent, and suddenly, my mouth went agape. No way. This was not happening. I mean, I had heard him being killed. We had all heard him being mauled. There was absolutely no way this could be happening. But there he was, coming out of the tent, unscathed, and slowly walking up to me. Without saying a word, he just stared at me for a good three to four seconds, as if he saw something he had never seen before. Henk, breathing heavily, was still scanning the whole campsite, looking for our hairy killer visitors. I stared back at Jerry and screamed softly, "What the hell!"

Without saying a word, he just shook his head, turned around, and slowly walked back to his tent. As I slowly began to comprehend, I heard some rustling noises coming from the small acacia tree by the Boma's fence. I looked up into the tree that could have easily been just about two and a half metres tall with a couple of lower branches armed with the sharpest thorns I had seen. Amongst the few branches were two that sort of leaned towards its right side, one on top of the other, and my eyes could not believe what I saw. Richard was sitting on the top branch, while Steve, who could have easily weighed over 100 kg was perched up on the lower branch. How the small tree managed to carry the both of them without collapsing is still a mystery to me. At first, I had thought they were rangers sent by the lodge manager to assist us after hearing the noises, but realised they were our own.

Still awestruck, I managed to say, "How the hell did you do that?" They quietly started negotiating their way down through the menacing thorns.

"How the hell did you guys get up there?"

I found myself asking again.

The funny thing is, it had taken these two a fraction of a second to climb up to the top of this thorny tree, but climbing down took them ten minutes because of the formidable thorns.

Well, I guess survival was more important than a couple of scratches, especially when visited by lions. So I'm sure right now you are all wondering, what the hell had just happened? In brief, Jerry, who had never in his life stayed on a wild campsite like this had a nightmare in which lions had entered his tent, thanks to Henk for teasing him about lions going for the weak, and started mauling him. The whole thing was just a dream. There were no lions in camp. The something that had zipped past me like a jet was Steve on his way to the tree.

The next morning, under his feet, there were blisters the size of a golf ball from stepping on hot coals while making for the tree.

Well, eventually, we all went back to bed, me and Steve in my tent, the white boys still slept outside on their stretcher beds, with the light off; white people.

Jerry did not get the job, the reason the HR gave him was, "Imagine you having that kind of a nightmare on an actual safari and sending twenty clients scurrying off into the night where there might be real hungry lions."

The tree climber, Richard, did not get the job, bad luck, I guess.

Steve, I guess, was lucky. He still works for the company today.

As for me, as I lay down, back in the safety of my tent, I told myself that this had been one hell of a night. I checked my time, it was four a.m., just two hours before we had to get up again. I closed my eyes and drifted off.

Chapter 9
In Bed with the Jungle Queen

When I woke up to prepare coffee, tea, and biscuits that cold morning in one of the wildest bush camps in Masai Mara National Park in Kenya, I wasn't aware that I was about to witness a miracle no living human being I knew had ever witnessed. The camp was full. I could count five overland trucks (a big truck, custom built to carry tourists) and several 4x4 land cruisers. It was still about forty-five minutes before sunrise, and only cooks were up and already busy with breakfast preparations. Clients would soon start emerging from their tents, most of them for quick toilet visits, as they would have been too scared to go during the night.

Being from Southern Africa, and not yet fluent in the Swahili language, I had not joined the Kenyan drivers and cooks for a drink at one of their campsites the previous night. I had chosen to sit with my twenty-one clients by our fire, sharing memories of that afternoon's sightings, and I remember hearing them talk and laugh loudly, long after we had all gone to bed. This morning, as I was busy with breakfast preparation for my clients, I overheard one of the Kenyan cooks say, "Don't wake him up. Want to see his face when he wakes up to find everybody standing around an empty table." He was referring to the cook of the truck furthest from me, who, apparently had overslept in his tent. From where I was standing, I could clearly see his tent, which seemed slightly open.

A warning bell sounded faintly at the back of my mind but quickly faded away.

This was mean, I thought to myself, but there was nothing I could do as I wasn't familiar with how they joked. As it was getting lighter and lighter, clients started coming out of their tents, some rushing to the bathroom while some started fixing themselves some coffee and tea, amid an exchange of morning greetings. It was suddenly getting louder in the camp, but still no sign of the Kenyan coming out of his tent. Even his clients started emerging from their tents.

Now, whenever possible, the crew always pitch their tents as far away from their clients as possible, for several reasons; the most common one being, they can come and go anytime without making noise for their clients, especially, since they always go to bed last, and are the first ones up early in the morning. The missing cook's tent was about thirty or so metres from his client's, and not very far from the bush line; probably why their noises could not wake him up. Just as I was about to go tent to tent, announcing coffee and tea were ready, something caught my eye, a slight shaking movement of the Kenyan cook's tent. I paused and watched in horror as a lion's big, round head appeared from the tent. I literally froze and could only yell out the word, lion! Everyone looked towards me, followed my gaze, and just froze like me. The lion pulled back into the tent and, a few moments later, stepped out of the tent, followed by three little cubs that could have easily been eight weeks old. She paused in front of the tent, stared at us for about three seconds, and then looked down at her cubs as if to say, let's go, then together they slowly walked around to the back of the tent and disappeared into the tall yellow grass.

My open mouth had gone so dry 1 couldn't feel my own tongue. My heart was pounding loudly I thought those near me could hear it. I remember one of my clients had been taking pictures of the lioness. There was total silence in the camp as everyone tried to come to terms with what they had just witnessed. The other Kenyan cooks had not said a word or moved an inch since I had screamed, "Lion."

From the corner of my eye, I saw them glance at each other and nod. But before anyone could walk up to the tent, two hands slid out of it, pushed the flaps apart, and the cook got out. His eyes went straight to his truck, where his clients stood, staring at him in disbelief. Without saying anything to anyone, he rushed to his truck's kitchen side and started opening lockers and pulling out food crates, loudly placing them on the table. It was like watching a ghost. Using the matches he pulled out of his shorts pocket, he lit the gas stove and placed a kettle full of water on it. Then he suddenly got really mad at his friends for not waking him up.

From the little Swahili I could pick up, they were telling him about lions in his tent. He told them to stop the stupid jokes and know that they were bad friends and that their friendship was over. Some of his clients, who had now recovered from the shock, started telling him about the lions too, but he still brushed them aside, that is when John, my client that had taken pictures, and I walked over to the cook. John showed him the lion pictures, and at that moment, the cook looked at his tent, back at the pictures on John's camera screen, and understood. A look of utter horror clouded his face before his knees buckled under him and he collapsed right there in front of us, his eyes rolling back as his body stretched out on the ground. His driver, who also had not woken up, came out of the truck's cabin and walked over to us. The other Kenyans explained to him what had just happened. He just stood there, his eyes wide with fear.

About three hundred metres from this camp is a small compound for rangers who are on standby to assist should something like this happen in the camp. They arrived a few minutes later, put the cook in their Land Rover, and took him to the park's clinic to be treated for shock. As this was our last day in the park, we quickly broke camp, packed up, and drove towards the main exit. I was thinking hard. There was only one explanation for what had happened, and this is what I think had happened.

The previous night, drunk as a skunk, the cook had entered his tent, forgot to close it, and passed out. The lioness with her cubs walked by, in the early hours of the day, and it being a cold night, they had gotten into the tent, probably thinking it was a cave, and snuggled up to the warm dead log. The guy was saved by being a soundless sleeper who also did not move around in his sleep, because had he moved, that would have been his demise. The smell of alcohol may have drowned his scent, preventing the lion from picking it up. The growing noises from us must have woken her up, prompting her to investigate. When she peeped out the door and saw us, she quickly told the cubs it was time to move.

Now, think about this, when the Kenyan cook's friends thought they were fixing him, they were actually saving his life, for, had they gone over to his tent and tried waking him up, either by calling out his name, shaking his tent or opening the tent door, the lion would have reacted, first by attacking the bigger threat; the guy in the tent.

Sometimes when we kick a frog, we are helping him cross the river.